Mercuri Kongress AB proudly presents

COLIN MOON

SMORGASBORD? I ORDERED APPLE
THIS IS SWEDEN, NOT EDEN

This book is dedicated to Solbritt,
Swedish sunshine personified.

Author's note

The masculine pronoun 'he' has been used when referring to the Swede. This is to avoid awkward language such as 'he/she', 'him/her', 'his or her'. No sexual prejudice or discrimination is intended.

A FEW WORDS WITH THE AUTHOR

OK, so why another book about Swedes?
There's so much to say. They never cease to amaze and amuse me. And I quite like them.

What do you like most about living in Sweden?
I've learnt the names of insects. For me before they were just horrible little bastards that bite. In the garden of SwEden they have names like *mygg*, *bromsar* and *knott*. Swedes also know the names of trees.

First insects and now trees?
I was born in south-east London and there we had two types of tree – a tree and a Christmas tree. And that was usually plastic. In Sweden they pick up a leaf and can tell you immediately if it's a leaf from a woople-doople tree or a hurdy-gurdy tree.

Anything else?
The singer, Lena Philipsson.

Lena Phil...?
I'm in love. Oh, and the actor Mikael Persbrandt.

That'll confuse the readers. What's the best thing about Swedes?
Their teeth.

I beg your pardon?
Swedes in general have nice teeth. I'm British and our teeth are as bad as our plumbing.

How Swedish have you become?
I hope one day to become normal just like the Swedes. I now start thinking about the coming weekend as early as Wednesday afternoon and I dress warmly in April even if there is a heat wave. It is, after all, only April. My pronunciation of *sjut-tio-sju* has been highly praised and my singing of *Helan går* has been warmly applauded.

Was it easy to learn Swedish?
I'm still learning how to pronounce it. I get my dots mixed up sometimes and say I'm off out to feed the widows instead of the ducks (*änkor/ankor*). And I sexually harass my neighbours when I should bump into them (*stöta* ***på****/****stöta*** *på*).

What about being 'lagom'?
I think I felt *lagom* once, one afternoon in November in Sheleftyou.

You mean Skellefteå.
Right. I was there once. Nice place. But it rained. It was like being in a car wash for a week.

How do you cope with the climate?
Well actually, I quite like rain. At least you don't have to shovel it. I was brought up with it. Swedes always talk about the weather. It's a safe subject to talk about. And anything that is safe is fine with Swedes. See the zipper on these trousers? It was a Swede who invented it. And you can't get much safer than that, can you?

After all these years in Sweden you must have got used to most things Swedish by now.
I can't manage Swedish measurements. Wine comes in 75 cl, cream as 3 dl, so what on earth is 500 ml?

The author on Swedish Television singing a well-known drinking song – the glass contains pure Swedish tap water.

Right, we're running out of time. How long are you going to stay in Sweden?
Forever and ever, Amen. Well, at least till I'm 65 anyway. I've bought a private pension insurance and for the benefit of any age-fixated Swedes reading this I am not there yet.

Thank you Colin, 50.

MEETINGS

Three things in Sweden are certain: death, taxes and more meetings.

Until I came to Sweden I was under the distinct and very naive impression that meetings were meant to produce decisions. I have since learnt that the purpose of a Swedish meeting is to find out whether or not you are at the meeting in order to decide when the meeting will be held in which you will decide when you will meet to talk about what happened at your meeting.

Meetings are short but many and are intended to give Bengan, Maggan and Lasse a chance to say what they think. If you want to reach a decision then you'll have to arrange another meeting because in the meantime Bengan, Maggan and Lasse have to go back to the office and ask Ninni, Kicki and Titti (yes, there *are* girls of that name) what *they* think.

Involved

This, in Swedish, is called the *förankringsprocess*. There's a process for everything. This one means getting everybody involved in everything forever. When a Swede says anything with the word 'process' on the end, you know that the whole procedure is going to take some time.

Meetings turn into a festival of consensus. This means that people can agree that they don't agree about anything. But what they will agree on is the exact time and date of the next meeting.

Other than that, the one thing to come out of a Swedish meeting is usually the people themselves.

> **"We are going to continue to have these meetings every day until I find out why we are not reaching our targets."**
>
> A SWEDISH BOSS TAKES ACTION.

AGENDAS

Swedes stick strictly to agendas.

They *prickar av* –'tick off' (not prick off) each point after everybody has taken turns discussing it. They move swiftly through the agenda as they all have another meeting planned ten minutes after this one has finished. They intensely dislike the last point on the agenda which is *övriga frågor* – 'any other business'. It's there just for good form. No self-respecting Swede wants to be guilty of causing the meeting to run over time. There is a distinct danger that 'any other business' could drag on and flexibility is not a Swedish strong point. Anybody having a spontaneous question or having saved

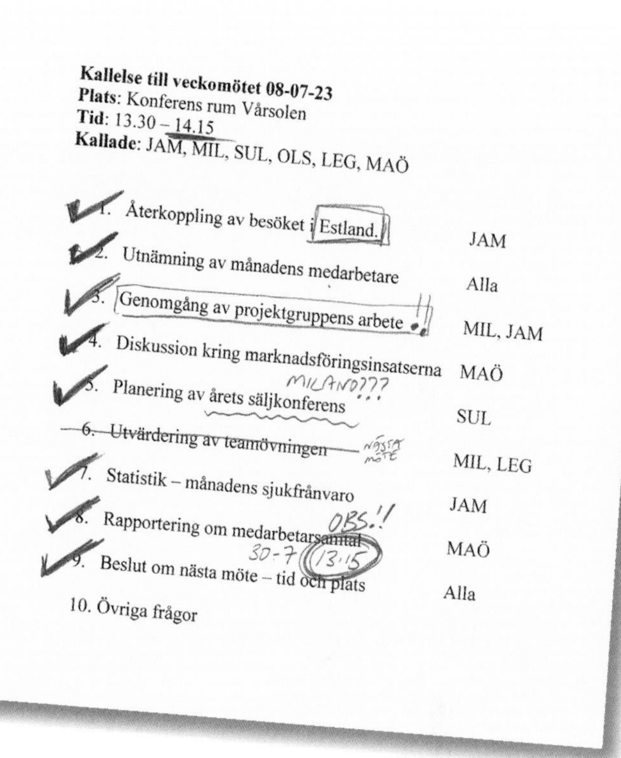

Kallelse till veckomötet 08-07-23
Plats: Konferens rum Vårsolen
Tid: 13.30 – 14.15
Kallade: JAM, MIL, SUL, OLS, LEG, MAÖ

1. Återkoppling av besöket i Estland.	JAM
2. Utnämning av månadens medarbetare	Alla
3. Genomgång av projektgruppens arbete	MIL, JAM
4. Diskussion kring marknadsföringsinsatserna	MAÖ
5. Planering av årets säljkonferens	SUL
~~6. Utvärdering av teamövningen~~	MIL, LEG
7. Statistik – månadens sjukfrånvaro	JAM
8. Rapportering om medarbetarsamtal	MAÖ
9. Beslut om nästa möte – tid och plats	Alla
10. Övriga frågor	

an exciting issue until this stage is probably a foreigner. You know, the ones who are always late and mess up schedules.

> **"Twenty-three minutes past. In precisely seven minutes Luigi will be late."**
>
> SWEDISH DELEGATE AND THE FINAL COUNTDOWN.

DECISIONS

Sweden didn't do much during the Second World War and they did that pretty well.

Swedes stayed more or less neutral (mostly less as it turns out) and let the rest of Europe fight it out among themselves. Even today, in many European countries, people still ask the question 'What did your grandfather do in the Second World War?' A Swede can simply answer 'He sat around in a sauna and ate crispbread.'

I come from a country that never says no to a good war, provided it's held in someone else's country. But Swedes are right, as usual: it's not nice fighting, as people can get hurt. Having said that, I note that the Swedes have a pretty impressive record themselves when it comes to war. They were good at giving the Danes and the Russians a tough match now and then. Since the reign of Gustav Wasa they have taken part in no fewer than 31 wars. They lost 10, drew 3 and won a notable 18.

Neutrality

In 1812 they officially turned neutral. Or did they? Perhaps they did. Or maybe no. On the other hand it depends.

All this neutrality has had an effect on modern-day Swedes. They can at times be rather indecisive when they're not too sure. A couple of hundred years of neutrality has taught Swedes not to take sides. Well, not until they know who's going to win anyway. This means that instead of saying *ja* or *nej* they say *nja* which means 'yes-but-no-but-yes-but'.

You may wonder how on earth they ever make a decision. Business Swedes themselves have sometimes called this *beslutsimpotens* – which, I suppose, means not having the balls to decide one way or another. Swedes believe that time is quality in decision making. Let us decide once and for all that, once committed, the Swedes are the most sincere, reliable people to deal with. Perhaps.

> **"Let me have some time to think about it. I'm not really sure. It depends. What I can do now is give you a definite maybe."**
>
> SWEDISH BOSS.
> THE SWEDISH DECISION-MAKING PROCESS TAKES TIME.

WORK ETHIC

Sweden is full of willing people – some willing to work and others willing to let them.

Most Swedes are constantly trying to find a healthy work-life balance. Work is a fine thing if it doesn't take up too much spare time. They might say they work hard; it's just that they are not often **at** work to do it.

Look in a Swedish diary and you may get the impression that no one in this country is ever at work. Try to get hold of someone on a Friday afternoon and this will be confirmed. Swedes will start to ask you about your plans for the coming weekend as early as Wednesday afternoon. By Friday lunchtime they have mentally *gått för dagen* – 'left for the day'.

Public holidays

The Swedes have a fair share of public holidays. In a good year they take as many days off in May and June as most Americans take in a year. And they still have their five weeks' vacation to take out when it suits them. Not only do they have 'red days' as the Swedes call their official holidays, but they may be given half the day off before, just to get them into the holiday mood. If they've planned it well they can take out a *klämdag* or two, which are odd days between a holiday and the weekend. In May, June and July the weekends and public holidays more or less combine into one long vacation with the occasional day at the office.

Aftonbladet
Onsdag 4 januari 2006

11

Har du kläm på helgerna i år?

Tillbaka på jobbet efter julledigheten – och redan semestersugen?

Ta det lugnt, 2006 kan bli ett vinnarår för vila.

Så får du din ledighet att räcka längre

Det har varit snålt med lediga dagar de senaste åren. Helgerna har legat på veckosluten och semesterdagarna har tagit slut fort. Men nu vänder den negativa trenden. 2006 innebär två extra lediga dagar, och med lite trixande i kalendern kan du få långledigt flera gånger under året.

Långledigt i påsk

För bara tre och en halv semesterdag får du tio dagars vila över påsken, som i år ligger i mitten av april. Tar du dess-

Här lyfts Thomas Bruno ur lergropen i träsket. Foto: AP

Ville ha sex – fastnade i träsket

NEW YORK. Thomas Bruno hade tänkt sig att inleda året med ett möte med en manlig prostituerad.

Istället fastnade han i en lergrop – och fick räddas med helikopter.

Bruno, 49, hade blivit osams med den tilltänkte älskaren i Rehoboth Beach

A Swedish newspaper tells you all the ways of getting as much time off work as possible.

Whoever said Swedes weren't flexible? By starting work at 6.30 each morning Swedes can clock up enough hours for a free Friday afternoon. 51 % of Swedish employees with children work at places where flexitime is part of the normal working day. 38% take advantage of it regularly compared to an average of 20% in the rest of Europe.

6 June

The Swedes now have a public holiday on their national day, 6 June. Nobody quite knows why, or what they're supposed to do. At least Swedes know what to do at Midsummer which, in people's minds, will forever be the most Swedish of all holidays. They erect a pole which looks a little like a phallic totem pole and dress it in branches, twigs and flowers and spend the afternoon dancing around it pretending to be small frogs.

However, fair's fair – when they're at work they're very efficient. But not before 8.30 as they have flexi-time, and not after 4 pm, thank you, as they have to pick up the kids from play school, and not after 2 pm on Fridays, if you don't mind, and preferably not between 1 May and 10 August.

COFFEE BREAKS

If Swedes skipped their coffee breaks they could retire five years earlier.

I come from a country where the coffee tastes like a chemistry experiment. Swedes, on the other hand, have the best coffee in the world. They drink litres of it from the moment they get up until 6 pm when they abruptly stop. The theory is that although you've been drinking oceans of the stuff all day the one cup you drink after 6 pm will keep you awake all night.

Coffee is an integral part of any meeting, either as an on-going self-service affair during the discussions or as a separate break. The coffee break is not to be confused with the briefer, more frequent leg-stretcher. I was once asked by a seminar participant if the group could have a 'bone-stretcher'. The words for leg and bone are the same in Swedish. On another occasion I was asked if I wanted a 'leg-spreader'.

EVERYDAY SWEDISH
Lesson 1

Hej, hej!	hay hay	(Literally: hello, hello or goodbye, goodbye) *Are you coming or going?*
Läget?	lay-get?	(Lit: The situation?) *And may I inquire as to your health this fine morning?*
Det är skitgott	deh eh sheetgott	(Lit: It's as good as shit) *It's simply superb!*

TIME

Modern day Swedes are still slaves to time.

Long-term planning with a purpose is the name of the game. Want to make a Swede panic? Suggest a spontaneous, sudden, free half-hour walk without any specific destination. Swedes don't like to waste time, they like to spend it and manage it. They like to be in time and on time. They like to *hinna*, a word which means to organise things so that they have enough time to do something properly. The Swedish concept of a personal failure can be expressed with the words *jag hann inte* – 'I didn't organise my time well enough to do things properly'.

> **"The trouble with being punctual is that there is very rarely anyone there to appreciate it."**
>
> SWEDISH BUSINESSMAN WORKING ABROAD.

Time to live

In my early days I once offered a Swedish acquaintance visiting my apartment a glass of wine. He immediately looked at his watch. He then, hesitatingly, said: 'It is only Thursday, but, oh well, you only live once'. It struck me as odd that he had looked at his watch before deciding to only live once. I have since noticed that this often happens – offer them something reasonably alcoholic on a day they're not expecting it and Swedes will look at their watch. Try it.

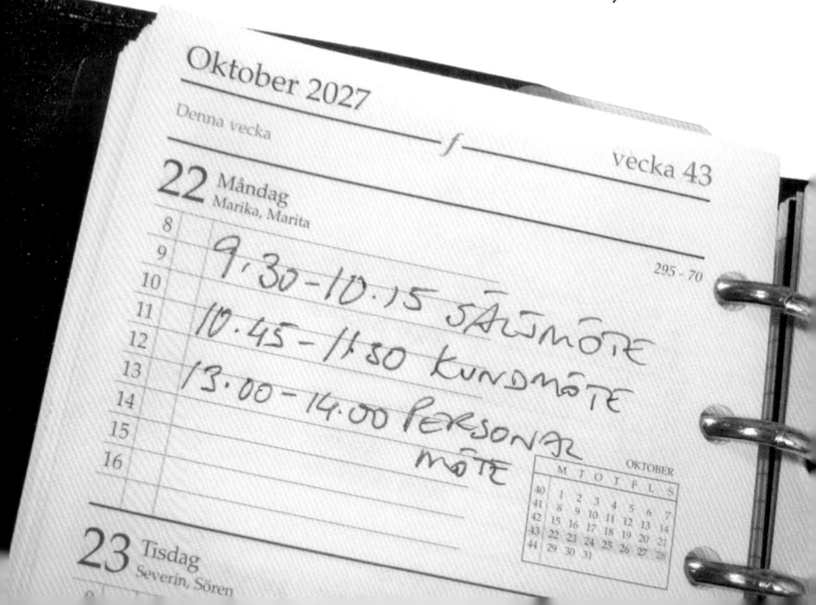

JOBS

Within 30 seconds of meeting a Swede he will ask you what you do for a living.

Every culture on earth has a system of classifying people, putting people in categories – subjectively or objectively – based on background, religion, appearance, sex etc. In Sweden they do it too. They put people in a *fack*, which is the unfortunate Swedish word for category.

Swedes are very interested in your line of business. Depending on your answer you can be put into any one of the following categories:

- the 'rich but dishonest' *fack* (a *VD* which is the unfortunate Swedish word for company director)
- the 'you're all out to fiddle your taxes' *fack* (self-employed, small company owner)
- the 'OK but you'll never make the break' *fack* (pre-school teacher, assistant nurse)
- the 'let's feel sorry for you' *fack* (office cleaner, check-out assistant)
- the 'it's a good enough job for a foreigner so stop complaining' *fack*, (station platform sweeper, taxi driver)

- the official 'oh dear' or unofficial 'get off your backside and work' *fack* (those on early sickness retirement benefits, the unemployed).

NAMES

In some cultures the two-part family name is a sign of aristocratic breeding. In Sweden it is a sign of political correctness.

Women tend to keep their maiden names and then attach their husband's name on the end with or without a hyphen (-). To be even more politically correct, the modern man keeps his name and tags his wife's family name on the end of that. In single-sex marriages it's of course the same principle – his name then his husband's. The Swedish love of two-part first names means that names become quite a mouthful: Anna-Kristin Sjölander-Börjesson and Björn-Åke Tidelius-Stormfalk. Swedish e-mail addresses are half the length of the mail itself. By the time you have finished writing in the address it would have been quicker to phone:

jan-erik.ahnberg-lindstrom@swedishcompany.se

or

maria.pia.forsgren-galfvensjo@anotherswedishfirm.se

In Sweden it's possible to find out how many people share a particular name. At the time of writing, 276 131 are called Johansson – the most common family name in the country. The name Svensson is in 9th place with 111 175 people.

I can thus tell you that there are surprisingly 471 men in this country with the name Colin and 360 of these, including myself, use it as their given name. What is more surprising is that there are 27 people with the family name Moon.

AGE

Swedes are also particularly interested in other people's age.

Stina, 56, tells of her frightening ordeal. Stina was locked up at gunpoint with a madman for two days at a currency exchange office in central Stockholm. Her age is of such great importance that it's in nice big black letters in the headline. We don't really care what happened to her as long as we

10 GISSLAN

– Jag tvi

Stina, 56, berättar om skräcktimmen

Rånaren ville släppa Stina Lerbacka, 56.

Men hon vägrade överge sin unga kollega.

– Min väninna sa att hon aldrig skulle glömma mitt beslut, säger Stina Lerbacka.

Först efter påtryckningar från polisen lämnade hon fångenskapen.

Det har gått tolv timmar sedan rånaren och gisslantagaren gett upp och överlämnat sig till polisen på Centralstationen i Stock-

– Han viftade lite med pistolen och pekade på någonting han hade på bröstet och sa "bomb, bomb". Mer än så var det inte.

Kvinnorna fick röra sig fritt i lokalen. De fick hämta vatten när de ville. Efter en timme sa mannen åt Stina Lerbacka att hon inte såg frisk ut och kunde gå om hon ville.

– Jag sa att jag inte överger min väninna.

know how old she was. If you missed the headline, her age is repeated in the very first sentence. If you have a short memory, don't worry. Her age is confirmed half way down the first page. The article is so long (pages 10, 11, 12, 13, 15, 16 and 17) it's a wonder Stina hasn't turned 57 by the end if it.

TAX

I am proud to be paying taxes in Sweden. But I could be just as proud for half the money.

According to the OECD over 50% of Sweden's GDP (gross domestic product) goes in taxes. Everything has a tax smacked on it, or a hefty VAT (moms) tag. I once heard though, that the authorities were considering abolishing VAT on funerals. That way the population would have something to look forward to – *att dö momsbefriat,* to die free of VAT.

When it comes to filling in their tax forms, many Swedes try to cheat successfully without really lying. Although they themselves may not always be 100% honest, they sure expect everyone else to be. It's called solidarity. We can all share as long as someone else pays.

Each year the evening newspapers print page after page with complete details of the income, tax bills and wealth status of the rich and famous. It's a veritable orgy of envy! The less tax they have paid, the more indignant other Swedes become. The wealthy politician who manages to end up with a modest tax bill of 60% instead of 80% is in for a tough ride.

However, I do know of a way to escape the anger of the people for not paying your fair share of taxes. Jump two metres over a high pole in international athletics, hit a tennis ball back and forth at Wimbledon or ski down a slope in Austria. Win a medal, do it for the glory of Sweden and nobody will even mention the word *skattesmitare* (tax evader) when you move to Monaco.

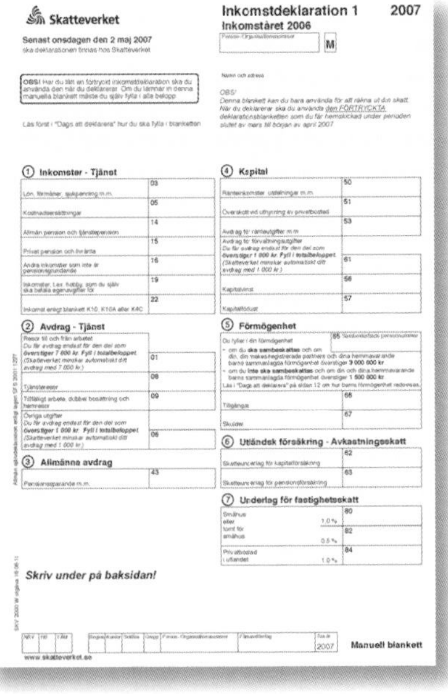

Skatteverket

Inkomstdeklaration 1 **2007**
Inkomståret 2006

Senast onsdagen den 2 maj 2007
ska deklarationen finnas hos Skatteverket

M

OBS! Har du fått en förtryckt inkomstdeklaration ska du använda den när du deklarerar. Om du lämnar in denna manuella blankett måste du själv fylla i alla belopp.

Läs först i "Dags att deklarera" hur du ska fylla i blanketten

Namn och adress

OBS!
Denna blankett kan du bara använda för att räkna ut din skatt. När du deklarerar ska du använda den FÖRTRYCKTA deklarationsblanketten som du får hemskickad under perioden slutet av mars till början av april 2007

① Inkomster - Tjänst

Lön, förmåner, sjukpenning m.m.	03
Kostnadsersättningar	05
Allmän pension och tjänstepension	14
Privat pension och livränta	15
Andra inkomster som inte är pensionsgrundande	16
Inkomster, t.ex. hobby, som du själv ska betala egenavgifter för	19
Inkomst enligt blankett K10, K10A eller K4C	22

② Avdrag - Tjänst

Resor till och från arbetet *Du får avdrag endast för den del som* ***överstiger 7 000 kr. Fyll i totalbeloppet.*** *(Skatteverket minskar automatiskt ditt avdrag med 7 000 kr.)*	01
Tjänsteresor	08
Tillfälligt arbete, dubbel bosättning och hemresor	09
Övriga utgifter *Du får avdrag endast för den del som* ***överstiger 1 000 kr. Fyll i totalbeloppet.*** *(Skatteverket minskar automatiskt ditt avdrag med 1 000 kr.)*	06

③ Allmänna avdrag

Pensionssparande m.m.	43

④ Kapital

Ränteinkomster, utdelningar m.m.	50
Överskott vid uthyrning av privatbostad	51
Avdrag för ränteutgifter m.m.	53
Avdrag för förvaltningsutgifter *Du får avdrag endast för den del som* ***överstiger 1 000 kr. Fyll i totalbeloppet.*** *(Skatteverket minskar automatiskt ditt avdrag med 1 000 kr.)*	61
Kapitalvinst	56
Kapitalförlust	57

⑤ Förmögenhet

Du fyller i din förmögenhet
- om du **ska sambeskattas** och om din, din make/registrerade partners och dina hemmavarande barns sammanlagda förmögenhet överstiger 3 000 000 kr
- om du **inte ska sambeskattas** och om din och dina hemmavarande barns sammanlagda förmögenhet överstiger 1 500 000 kr

Läs i "Dags att deklarera" på sidan 12 om hur barns förmögenhet redovisas.

Tillgångar	66
Skulder	67

⑥ Utländsk försäkring - Avkastningsskatt

Skatteunderlag för kapitalförsäkring	62
Skatteunderlag för pensionsförsäkring	63

⑦ Underlag för fastighetsskatt

Småhus eller	1,0 %	80
tomt för småhus	0,5 %	82
Privatbostad i utlandet	1,0 %	84

Skriv under på baksidan!

2007

Manuell blankett

www.skatteverket.se

The Swedish deklarationsblankett *(tax form). This will soon be a historic document as in the near future Swedes will be able to do it over the net or, believe it or not, via a text message on their mobiles. Although Swedes produce a lot of paper, they often find ways of not having to use it.*

Att betala skatt är häftigt! "It's great to pay tax!"
ONE PROMINENT SWEDISH POLITICIAN ENCOURAGES SWEDES TO LET THE STATE GET HOLD OF THEIR MONEY BEFORE THEY START TO SPEND IT.

MONEY

Money is to Swedes what sex is to the British – rather disgusting but at the same time somewhat exciting.

Sweden is a capitalist country without capitalists. It's not good taste to brag too much about how financially successful you are. There are other things in the garden of SwEden which are naturally more important – like picking berries or singing in choirs. As a Swede you're expected to say: *jag bryr mig inte så mycket om pengar* – 'I'm not fussed about money'. A sensible Swede called Jerker (yes, there are Swedes with that name too) told me once that money wouldn't buy me happiness. I told him: 'Jerker, it's not happiness I want – it's money.' There followed a silence longer than one of Ingmar Bergman's loaded dramatic pauses. As a Swede he was stunned that someone could say such a thing.

The standard of living in Sweden is quite high. It's just a shame that many Swedes can't afford it.

People try as hard as they can to live within their income even if they have to borrow from the bank to do so. The cost of living works out as approximately income plus ten per cent.

> **"Personally I don't mind that they closed my bank. At most they only ever had two or three cashiers, except when they were busy at lunchtime, and then they had one."**
>
> AN INTERNET USER. BANKS HAVE CLOSED MANY OF THEIR BRANCHES AS SWEDES PREFER TO DO THEIR TRANSACTIONS AT HOME.

Euro's a flop

SWEDES were fuming last night after their country was depicted as a limp **WILLY** on the new euro coins.

Brussels insiders are mischievously claiming that euro chiefs deliberately set out to humiliate Sweden for staying out of the single currency, like Britain and Denmark.

The embarrassing image is the result of Sweden's neighbour Norway, a non-EU country, being cut out of a map on the coins.

● **GERMAN** Chancellor Gerhard Schroeder faces being booted out at polls in September as voters show their fury over jobless figures of four million – the result of preparing the country's economy for the euro.

EU member . . image of Sweden on coin shows euro is a soft currency

The Sun newspaper (3 million copies sold per day) knows why the Swedes voted no in the referendum on whether or not to adopt the Euro.

EVERYDAY SWEDISH
Lesson 2

Messa mig	messa may	(Approx: Mess me) *Please text me at your convenience.*
Den är jätteliten!	den eh yetteleeten	(Lit: It is gigantically small) *You have such an itsy-bitsy thing, almost invisible to the human eye.*
Det knallar och går	deh knallar ock gore	(Lit: It bangs and walks) *Life is just jogging along in a most hunky-dory fashion.*

SERVICE

'Service' is one of those words that Swedes needed to import.

You get good service in Sweden. They have done particularly well with the concept of 'self-service'. If you want it, do it yourself. If brothels were legal in Sweden, believe me they'd be self-service too.

There are some companies, however, that have adopted the word service but have unfortunately forgotten to import the concept that goes with it. Suppose your house has burnt down. You would

"Oh no, it's the vikings! And they've brought their bloody self-assembly furniture with them!"

Self-service Swedish style. Swedes have successfully exported the concept of if-you-want-it-do-it-yourself to the whole world.

naturally ring for help. What you don't want to hear at that stage is a recording. The voice sounds as if the person behind it has left their brain on the bus: *Det är många som ringer just nu*. This, translated, means we have so many problems with our customers, or rather vice versa, that you haven't got a snowball's chance in hell of getting through.

In the telephone queue

You are then told you are number 63 in line, whether you like it or not, and that they will answer your call just as soon as they come back from their extended holiday. If you're really very lucky they will let you listen to piped music, the type which was played in your local supermarket at the beginning of the 1960s. Every thirty seconds a vaguely human voice lets you know you are still in the queue. When you have been reminded of this fact twenty times you begin to realise what it is like to get Chinese water torture. After what seems like three hours of wasted life, you hear that monotonous moron again: 'You are now number 59 in line'.

I once asked to speak to the head of customer service to explain my slight irritation at having to spend half the working week on and in their telephone line. I wanted to know just how come every time I called there were always at least 40 people ahead of me. The gentleman I spoke to, who sounded as bright as Helsinki in December, said: *Det är många som ringer…*

'No', I said, 'it's not that there are too many customers calling. There are too few people answering!' He offered me a *'Jaha…'* which, translated, means this smells like conflict so I'll just say *jaha*.

TEMPERATURE

Swedes call -10°C '10 degrees cold'. What then is 10°C? 10 degrees warm?

Winter is one of the coldest seasons in Sweden. If the Jews are God's chosen people then the Swedes are God's frozen people. They always feel the cold. Triple glazing, under floor heating and super-duper efficient central heating ensure that there is a regular room temperature of 22°C. Swedes can check it is regular by constantly monitoring the numerous thermometers hanging inside and outside every window in the house. No little stream of cool, fresh air ever finds its way indoors at any time because they then all complain: *Det drar!* They hate draughts as that's what you get in England and that's why little boys in short trousers have blue knees. So they tell me.

WEATHER

The forecast for tomorrow is partly cloudy, partly sunny, and partly accurate.

I have often wondered how they start conversations in hot countries where the weather is the same all year round. In Sweden there is so much weather, there's always something to talk about.

Att prata om vädret means to talk about the weather. However, *att prata väder* means to talk sheer, utter nonsense. Swedes constantly do one, but rarely the other.

> **"That's the end of the marvellous hot weather we've been having the past few weeks. Tomorrow there is once again a cold front coming in from the British Isles."**
>
> THE WEATHER-FORECASTER ALWAYS MAKES A POINT OF SAYING WHERE THESE COLD FRONTS COME FROM.

Swedes watch the weather forecast with great interest as they can prepare conversation openers for the following day. *De sa att det skulle bli regn* – 'They said it would rain' – is usually a good way to kick off a conversation. Everybody seems to know who 'they' are.

The climate in Sweden is changing, perhaps due to global warming. This means people are talking about the weather which has been more unusual lately than the usual unusual weather.

SEASONS

I like every season in Sweden. In winter I like the summer and in summer I like the winter.

Winter

The weather forecast for the night of 2 November to 23 February – dark.

No wonder some Swedes in the north are affected by SAD, which makes them just that, sad. SAD stands for seasonal affective disorder. Lack of natural daylight makes the thyroid hormone levels sink and to top it all, the circadian rhythms are badly affected. The senses are dulled and depression sets in and … well, you get the picture.

It sometimes seems as if the winter will never end.

Some northern Swedes get a fake sunshine fix by sitting in special 'light rooms' at the local hospital. Patients are dressed in white robes and sit in a glorious glow of lamps, basking for 2-3 hours at a time. This reminds them, of course, of what's to come – 100 days of uninterrupted daylight in the summer. Do not try this at home in your kitchen.

Spring

Swedes have a national wake-up call at around mid-March.

They wake up and promptly turn pagan. They stand erect and motionless with their backs against brick walls. They close their eyes tightly and point their faces at the sun. They are worshipping the sun god. Considering how many times they have been let down before, their faith in the sun-god seems pretty solid.

> **Me: "I got up at dawn this morning to see the sunrise."**
> **Friend "Well, you couldn't have picked a better time."**
>
> SWEDISH SARCASM – I LOVE IT.

Summer

The worst thing about the summer is that it comes so rarely.

The best thing about the summer in Sweden is that it is glorious! Swedish summer brings out the birds, the bugs and the beer drinkers. Born-again Swedes slap on their sunscreen and feel the urge to retreat, relax and recharge. At this time of year I wouldn't be anywhere else than in the beautiful, blooming garden of SwEden.

Noel Coward sang that mad dogs and Englishmen go out in the midday sun. In Sweden it's the half-dressed. Ignoring any dress codes or respectability they have observed during the rest of the year, some Swedes run around town semi-naked during the intense few weeks of the summer holiday. The standard of dress – or lack of it – can be rather eye-opening. If you're lucky you'll see plenty of beautiful, half-naked summer Swedes with delicious tan, smooth bodies and dazzling white teeth. If you're unfortunate you'll see Gun-Britt, 59, in her bikini top shopping at Willy's supermarket with her topless husband, Bengt-Åke.

> **"A few more summers like the one we've just had and we Swedes will start behaving like Italians."**
>
> REMARK DURING DINNER PARTY.

Autumn

Swedish mushrooms are to die for. (So pick the right ones).

Swedes grab a basket, a knife and a mushroom handbook and head into the woods. In the garden of SwEden chanterelles and mushrooms such as

Charles Johns (strangely called 'ceps' in English) grow in secret places. To find these succulent fungi is a matter of personal triumph. Swedes will gladly let you know where they found them – long after the mushroom season is over.

The Mushroom Song

If you go down to the woods today, you're sure of a big surprise.
They'll pick 'em, brush 'em, scrape 'em and save, you'll never believe your eyes.
For every Swede that ever there was, will gather there for certain, because,
It's autumn now and Swedes are picking their mushrooms.
Beneath the trees where nobody sees, you'll see them with their knives.
They'll hide and seek as long as they please, having the time of their lives.
For every Swede that ever there was, will gather there for certain, because,
They've found the spot, believe it or not, where they can pick their mushrooms.

(Sing to the tune of Teddybears' picnic)

MOSQUITOES

Sweden would have been a perfect place to live if Noah had refused to let the two mosquitoes board the ark.

If you ever think you are too small to make an impact, try being in a room at night with a mosquito. Strangely enough, no glossy tourist brochure about Sweden ever mentions mosquitoes but my conscience won't let me write a book about the garden of SwEden without mentioning them. They suck you dry of blood and swell up big enough to show on radar.

There are so-called fool-proof remedies for keeping the little bastards from bleeding you dry. For example smear yourself with garlic, shoe polish and cigarette ash. You might not frighten off too many mosquitoes but you'll keep the neighbours away for a few days.

Me: "I don't like all these mosquitoes".
Anders: "Well, just pick out the ones you like and I'll kill the rest."

AMUSING, ANDERS, VERY AMUSING.

EVERYDAY SWEDISH
Lesson 3

Men!	men!	(Lit: But!) *Excuse me, but how dare you simply push in the queue like that!*
aha upp-levelse	a ha oop-layvelser	(Approx: I have just experienced an aha!) *I have wondered about that all my life and have now finally got an answer to the mystery.*
Ja!	hah! (breathe abruptly inwards while saying it)	(Approx: I have asthma) *I couldn't agree with you more.*

THE ARTS

The creative arts are alive and kicking and most of it is exceedingly well done. But...

There is a wealth of Swedish films, theatre and television that is inspiring, inventive and innovative. After the USA and the UK, Sweden is the third largest exporter of music in the world. But...

Cinema

Entertainment in Sweden is sometimes a serious business. There are two things you'll never get from a Bergman film – *a*) a really good laugh, *b*) a decent car chase.

Bergman's idea of cinematic entertainment is dressing up some gloomy-faced specimen in a black sack, handing him a scythe, calling him Death and getting him to call round the neighbourhood as if asking to borrow a bowl of sugar.

In recent years there have been films such as 'F****** Åmål' about the complete waste of a youth spent in a hell-hole of a town where the kids are so depressed and disheartened that, watching it, you feel as helpless as the owner of a sick goldfish in its bowl.

My hero Mikael Persbrandt starred in a film called 'Night and Day'. The whole film is a close-up study of the said actor in his car driving round a rainy Gothenburg saying good-bye to everyone he knows. He tells you at the beginning of the film that he intends to end it all, and the way he drives you wonder why it hasn't happened sooner. By the time he actually does it, you feel as if you want to offer him a helping hand.

Theatre

How much human misery can you cram into a one and a half hour performance?

Lars Norén writes plays, the main ingredients

in which are despair, desolation, and depression. If they make it through the play, half the audience has been numbed into a coma and the other half is begging for the chance to commit suicide.

THE MEDIA

I will say what few Swedes ever say: I like SVT – Swedish Television.

Before

Swedish television has definitely improved over recent years. Right up until the early 1990s, however, Sweden only had two channels. Channel 1 was state propaganda and Channel 2 had a little flashing light in the top right hand corner of the screen telling you to turn back to Channel 1.

For years one of the biggest thrills at prime time was to watch *Anslagstavlan* – 'The Notice board'. It was full of government information on how to run your life, why you should eat 6-8 slices of bread per day, what not to eat, definitely what not to drink and anything else you weren't supposed to do if you wanted to live longer. Swedes were encouraged to give up smoking, drinking, and eating – they didn't actually live longer, it just seemed it. The mission of Swedish television was to show that life wasn't as much fun as you perhaps thought it was, and that you felt much worse than you thought you probably did.

SVT is the BBC of Sweden, and nowadays produces good quality television on a fraction of the BBC's budget. Having said that, I think there is still room for improvement.

Now

SVT offers a wide range of seemingly endless panel discussions and studio debates covering every topic imaginable. These discussion programmes are called 'Debate' and 'Argument', which is not bad for a people hell-bent on avoiding conflict and confrontation. The programmes are very popular – especially among the people who participate. Sweden has a hard core of five experts who appear in every other programme and voice their opinion. If only the whole world would just listen to them, then all the problems on the planet would be solved in 25 minutes.

There are a few home-made detective series produced to promote the myth that the Swedish police are good at solving crimes.

There are also one or two situation comedies – which are more situation than comedy. They all revolve around the *tönt*, a man, usually a misunderstood father, who has the IQ of about room temperature.

TV 4

The commercial channel TV4 has a staff of four – Martin, Malou, Agneta and Bengt. They have their own programmes and regularly turn up in each others'. They are probably overworked, presumably over-paid, and perpetually over-exposed.

TV 4 is remarkably clever at 'swedifying' foreign quiz show concepts and entertainment. Most of these shows revolve around the knock-out principle. They require the TV audience to ring in and vote like mad for their favourites. What with this, the commercials and the sponsors TV4 must be laughing all the way to the bank.

Many people get annoyed at the commercials interrupting the programmes. I get annoyed at the TV programmes interrupting the commercials. I see some pretty good acting on the commercials. Anyone who can get worked up over a plastic bottle of washing up liquid is a very good actor in my book.

Cable TV

Margareta Windbag, a former government minister, wanted to ban satellite dishes in the 1980s as she thought satellite TV would be a subversive influence on the innocent Swedish public. Nowadays Swedes have access to over 164 channels all showing back-to-back episodes of the Simpsons, the Nanny and Married with Children. On one of these channels they show the Swedish version of Big Brother, which proves that cable TV is a medium where people with nothing to do watch people doing it. The one thing all these channels have in common is killing time between the commercial breaks.

At the time we all thought Fru Windbag was insane.

EVERYDAY SWEDISH
Lesson 4

Det är dö'kul	deh eh der kool	(App: Death is fun). *This is the most hilarious experience I've had in a long time.*
Men hördudu!	men her-doohdooh	(Lit: But do you hear you) *Come to think of it…*
Men hallå!	men hallo!	(Lit: But hello!) *Are you stupid or what?*

Radio

SR (Swedish Radio) is to Swedes what the BBC is to the Brits – solid, reliable and as exciting as a long, stable marriage. There is some good quality broadcasting with news and views on P1, highbrow classics, with a dose of jazz and folk on P2, rap and crap on P3 and sport and local on P4.

The old communist block of Eastern Europe had commercial radio long before Sweden. Nowadays there are countless commercial radio stations, all of which offer the same music, jingles and gibberish. They take time out for a short piece of music and then get straight back to all the commercials.

Nej, det var inte bättre förr i Sverige, fast det är sämre nu. "No, things weren't better before in Sweden, even though it's worse now."

CALLER ON THE DAILY RADIO PHONE-IN – RING P1.

CRIME

Swedish criminals: with a little counselling they are expected to get over it.

Sweden, along with many other countries, has a problem with its crime rate. Perhaps they should get the Swedish tax authorities involved in crime solving as well? They could legalise it and then tax it out of business.

The Swedish police have never really recovered

from their failure to find Olof Palme's murderer. Their reputation for efficiency at that time was rather poor in the eyes of the world. It is said that Scotland Yard in London announced to their staff that they had some bad news and some good news. The bad news for everybody was that there was going to be an investigation into corruption within the police force. The good news for everybody was that they had asked the Swedish police to investigate.

FOOD

If the Bible had been written by a Swede there would have been a lot more recipes in it.

Indeed a well-known recipe book called *Sju sorters kakor* (Seven types of cake) is outsold only by the Bible. The biggest sellers in any bookshop are, however, not only the cookbooks but also the diet books. The cookbooks tell you how to cook the food and the diet books tell you how not to eat any of it.

You may wonder how I can have any opinion about other people's food, coming as I do from the UK. British food is delicious and perfectly safe as long as you don't get any of it in your digestive system. Swedish food, on the other hand, is perfectly safe to eat and Swedish cuisine is light years away from the early 70s. Then, the most exotic dish consisted of a chunk of ham with a slice of pineapple on it – something 'Hawaii' they called it. The noisiest food ever, Swedish crispbread, is now popular the world over. You can also find *Kalles kaviar,* which looks like Swedish toothpaste. The next thing, I understand, that the Swedes are keen to export is a delicacy called *lutfisk*. It is dried fish soaked in lye. It has absolutely no flavour – it's apparently rather like kissing your sister.

RUDE FOOD

It tastes better than it sounds.

A *semla* is rather like an almond paste cream burger, sold originally at Lent. It is sometimes called a *fastlagsbulle*. In my early days in the garden of SwEden I mixed up the two names and called it a *samlagsbulle*. Strictly translated it became an intercourse bun.

A delicacy on Thursdays is pea soup. Delicious!

Some Swedes refer to this in the less appetizing way as 'yellow pee soup'.

There are cookies which are long and narrow and are called *Finger Marie*. I kid you not. And Marie's not complaining.

There is a spice called *Kockens anis*, cat food called *Pussi* and a chocolate bar called *Plopp*. Feel free to explain to your Swedish friends why these are really quite amusing to the Anglo-Saxon ear.

FOOD SHOPPING

Limes, avocados and pistachio nuts are now everyday items on Swedish shopping lists, along with old faithfuls such as candles, dill-flavoured crisps, and 1 kg of pick'n'mix candy.

You can buy food with a clear conscience in Sweden as:

1. All Swedish meat comes from happy animals.
2. Most products are 'natural' if you are to believe the packaging – put on a picture of fields and flowers and Swedish consumers won't even look at the ingredients.
3. The TV commercial shows frisky dairy cows frolicking in the sunny

Reading the back of packets keeps Swedes busy at breakfast time. This carton of milk informs us that it is early spring in southern Sweden and cows are being released into the countryside from their winter imprisonment. Incredibly, there is a word for this in Swedish – 'betessläpp'.

This pig was happy according to the label Glad Gris *– well, at least it was until it had its heart ripped out.*

countryside before being locked up for nine months of the year due to the climate – which they conveniently don't mention.

You've heard about the high cost of living. In Swedish supermarkets it's the high cost of leaving that's the problem. Food is expensive. However, Swedish supermarkets are experts at making you believe you save money:

1. Swedes get a full 25 kronor bonus cheque after being forced to spend two thirds of their monthly income on expensive food and then pay 2 kronor for a plastic carrier bag to put it all in.
2. Swedes love *rabattkuponger* (no, not 'rabbit coupons' but discount coupons) and save 5 kronor on an article costing 150kr.
3. Food is expensive so Swedes look for things carrying an 'extra price'. This may sound

distinctly odd, but an *extrapris* in Swedish is in fact a lower price.

Den här juicen består av 100% naturliga apelsiner.
"This orange juice contains 100% natural oranges."

A SWEDISH ADVERTISEMENT. IS THERE SUCH A THING AS AN UNNATURAL ORANGE?

BEST BEFORE 1

Swedes don't seem to trust their noses and taste buds.

They go strictly by the best before date. Swedish bread has about four dates on it – the date they thought about baking it, the date when they baked it, the date by which it should be eaten and the date by which it should be thrown out to the birds. Once upon a time a Swedish food delegation to the EU tried to convince all those backward Europeans about the benefits of putting a whole range of dates on a loaf of bread, especially the 'eat before' date. After sitting through a 150 PowerPoint picture slide show enough to make you car sick, a confused Frenchman in the audience put up his hand and asked – 'Exsqueeze me? But in Sweden you eat **old** bread?' Case closed.

BEST BEFORE 2

Why is there an expiry date on a can of *surströmming*, a can of rotti ... fermenting fish?

QUEUE 1

Ask any Swede and they will tell you that they never miss an opportunity to stand in a queue.

But are they losing the art of spontaneous queuing, I wonder? It's all down to the queue ticket.

The queue ticket fits rather well into the Swedish way of doing things. It's organised, democratic, fair, efficient, and safe. Queue tickets, no larger than a postage stamp, sometimes provide you with three pieces of vital information. First, the number 37, your place in line. In the bottom right corner is the exact time, down to the milli-second, that you pulled the ticket out of the machine. In the bottom left corner is the approximate waiting time to get served. This is, of course, essential information for people who feel they need to do something constructive during those minutes they have to wait. Swedes who have time to spare immediately feel the need to fill it. It used to be called efficiency – now it's called stress. They rush out of that shop and into another and take yet another queue ticket. Number 87 and an estimated six minute wait. Enough time to make a few phone calls.

QUEUE 2

A Swede will, out of habit, sometimes take a queue ticket at a counter where there is clearly no-one else around. The solitary shop assistant, bored out of his mind, is just longing for someone to serve. The Swede, queue ticket in hand, forms an orderly queue of one. The assistant presses the button and the next number comes up on the display. And the Swede will actually look at the queue ticket to make sure it really is *his* turn.

QUEUE 3

Swedes may be willing to stand in a queue but they are not always as patient as they would like you to believe.

At the departure gate at the airport, Swedes in particular get ready to stand in a queue long before the word 'boarding' appears on the screen.

As soon as a check-in assistant arrives at the gate the remaining seated passengers start to fold their newspapers, gather their belongings and get up from their seat. One person moves in the vague direction of the gate and they're all up on their feet heading to form a queue. The incoming plane has just pulled into the gate and not yet dispersed its cargo of passengers, but that doesn't stop these queue-crazy passengers. Standing in this unnecessary queue for the next twenty minutes they subtly shuffle their feet forward at a pace of three centimetres a minute. This is particularly noticeable on domestic flights with unnumbered seating. Once the check-in assistant announces that they are ready to board there is one almighty surge forward. The queue crumbles into a mass of people all wanting to pass through the narrow bottle-neck of a gate at the same time. Don't count on hearing the Swedish equivalent of 'After you' too often.

QUEUE 4

It is not unusual in Sweden to queue up to take a queue ticket.

HEALTH

Ask Swedes how they are and they will tell you.

They may reply *jämna plågor* – constant aches and pains. If you're lucky you might get a *det knallar och går* – things are dragging along. This fascinates me as I come from a country where, if someone asks me how I am, I will, with the last dying breath in my body, say 'Fine thanks, and you?'

Between you and me Swedes tend to have a few too many aches and pains. If you tell them they suffer from hypochondria they're likely to say "Oh no, have I got that as well?"

These fit, outdoor-loving, sporty people always have something wrong with them. They'd be in much better health if they didn't insist on getting ill so much. You too can be as sick as a Swede.

Here are the most popular things to suffer from:

Be **hängig**
(Literally: hangy) – there are no specific things wrong with you, you just sort of hang around aimlessly, give in to gravity and let your body point southwards.

Be **allergic**.
Everyone can be allergic to something if they really think about it. Talk about your allergies at dinner. Everybody is very interested and will compare yours with theirs.

Be **vårtrött**
Extremely tired in the spring. When everything else is blooming, blossoming and bursting with life, be limp, lethargic and lacking in energy. Save enough strength to tell people all about it.

It is spring and Swedes need a cure for their anguish and anxiety. It is time to for them to be happy again. This newspaper hopes to sell a few extra issues by telling them how to go about it.

Suffer from **höstdepression**
Depression in the autumn/fall. After a refreshing, revitalising summer sink into despair and desolation. Look completely miserable and people will want to tell you how dreadful they usually feel in November too.

Suffer from **stress**
Have two or more things to do at once and get 'burnt out'. Or simply head 'straight for the wall'.

Be **halvtidssjukskriven**
This means that you are on the sick-list for half the time only. Sick for half the day and fit for the rest presumably.

Swedes will gladly talk about their aches and pains as many times as possible. Therefore the state health system is designed so that each time you go to the doctor's surgery you always meet a different doctor.

While it is free to go to the doctor's in some countries (Swedes won't believe you) in Sweden you have to pay a considerable amount. Having a sick family can be a costly affair – you hope that the youngest can wait a month with his flu as his big sister ate up the family's health budget last week with her ear infection.

> **"The human body, with proper care, will last a lifetime."**
>
> SWEDISH HEALTH CARE SENSE.

EVERYDAY SWEDISH
Lesson 5

Det beror på	deh beroar poh	(Lit: It depends on ...) *I really don't want to answer that.*
Med eller utan?	med eller ootan	(Lit: With or without?) *Do you want me to pay according to the stipulations laid down by the tax authorities or do you want an 'under-the-table' job?*
I mor'n ska jag vabba	ih monn ska ya vabba	(App: Tomorrow I shall be wabbing) *My child is going to be ill tomorrow so, horror of horrors, I'll have to stay at home from work.*

ROYALS

Guaranteed scandal-free.

The present king's ancestor King Karl XIV Johan was basically a transplanted French soldier who was asked if he wouldn't mind sitting on the throne of Sweden on the far away planet of Scandinavia.

The royal family is very popular. I was once introduced to the Queen at a major function. I was told she would be brought over to me. It was rather like being brought the dessert trolley in an expensive restaurant. She was just as delightful.

Swedes talk about the Royal Swedish Envy. I have never really understood this – who is the king envious of? Mind you, I am envious of him – his vintage cars, speedboats, free dinners and several pretty decent places to live.

> **"Do you have any ID?"**
>
> A SHOP ASSISTANT TO KING CARL XVI GUSTAV.

When they ask the King for his ID, he needs only show his crown.

DRINK

The Swedes have a complex attitude to alcohol. It's a product they hate to love.

Contrary to what people say, Swedes are not necessarily heavy drinkers – they can sometimes go for hours without touching a drop. They are currently 21st in the world alcohol consumption league – so they are officially not great drinkers. Swedes know that alcohol is a slow poison ... and they're in no hurry.

The Swedish state is terrified that its population will turn alcoholic given half the chance, so they export a lot of it before the Swedes can get their hands on it. Their biggest export is *Absolut,* so called for the absolute silence when it comes to the sheer hypocrisy of promoting and selling large quantities of alcohol to developing countries. Another up and coming export is Swedish beer, an intoxicating golden brew that re-emerges virtually unchanged an hour later.

Systembolaget

Over the past few years attitudes to alcohol have changed radically. A few years ago Swedes would lie on the beaches of Majorca, Rhodes and the Canaries on day two of their holiday discussing

what duty free booze they were going to buy on the way home. Now the *Systembolaget,* the state alcohol retail monopoly, has gone through a complete makeover. It is now a pure delight to go in and, service Swedish-style, serve yourself! Well, not exactly as it sounds, but they do now trust their customers to put a bottle or two into the basket without opening it before they get to the check-out desk.

Nowadays there is no longer the need to try to disguise the 'clunk clunk' sound of wine bottles on the bus on your way home. This used to be an audible sign that you were on the road to becoming an alcoholic. The popular three-litre bag-in-boxes make no sound at all so Swedes can shop and walk about with a clear conscience. The dull, narrow plastic bags for bottles and cans are still available. The state alcohol retail monopoly cleverly renamed them *miljöpåsar* – 'environment bags'. This means Swedes now unquestioningly pay for something which was free when it was just called a plastic bag.

> **"The best way to cure a hangover is to avoid alcohol the night before."**
>
> OVER THE YEARS THE STATE HAS LAUNCHED COUNTLESS CAMPAIGNS TO GET SWEDES TO DRINK LESS.

PETS

Animals in less civilised countries are potential food, carry infectious diseases or are a general pest. In Sweden they are considered fellow humans and are part of the family. They have high cholesterol, and weight and blood pressure problems – all the illnesses of the modern welfare state. The following conversation would not be unusual:

– How many are there in your family now?
– Well, there's me, Bengt, Pontus, Maria and Lizzie.
– Oh, you have three. How nice. How old is Lizzie?
– 14. She's a bit stiff in her limbs but she's a tough old bitch. We hope she'll survive another few years.

HUNTING

Swedes are true animal lovers as long as the animal answers to a name, can be stroked or lives in a stable. Otherwise it stands a very good chance of being shot.

While Swedes make a point of boycotting bullfighting in Spain because it is not a nice thing to do, over 250 000 of them have a moose hunting licence. They venture into the Swedish forests each autumn and pang – shoot dead a third of the 300 000 elk that roam this land.

18 AFTONBLADET KARTLÄGGER

AFTONBLADET KARTLÄGGER 19

De är bästa älgjägarna

Här är jaktlagen som sköt flest djur – i din kommun

Sveriges 15 i topp

FLER KVINNOR PÅ JAKT

Så läser du tabellen

Nässjö

Vaggeryd

Värnamo

Vetlanda

Sävsjö

Ödeshög

KALMAR LÄN

Emmaboda

Hultsfred

Högsby

Kalmar

Mönsterås

Page after page of the names of happy, heroic hunters and the number of moose they shot.

Full freezer

The pro-hunting lobby is powerful. Upsetting thousands of enthusiastically eager hunters is not a wise thing to do. They are already angrily saying *'Nej men ...!'* at this section of the book. And so are their friends and families who look forward to a freezer full of freshly shot elk each autumn. They have already stocked the *svartvinbärsgelé*, blackcurrant jelly, in anticipation.

Wearing fur coats or Canada Goose jackets with genuine fur trim will not necessarily get you splattered with red paint from animal activists in Sweden. After all, Swedish animals were happy when they had their brains blown out.

GOLF

Golf in Sweden is very popular.

> **"Golf and sex are the only two things Swedes can enjoy without being any good at them."**
>
> A SWEDISH GOLF-PLAYER WHO DOES A COUPLE OF THINGS JUST FOR THE PURE PLEASURE.

MOBILE/CELL PHONE

Everybody, even self-respecting 7 year-olds, has a cell phone.

I once wrote about the silent Swede. He has transformed into the screaming Swede. Give him a mobile and he'll shout into it. It's like giving him a megaphone. Nothing is sacred any more – love affairs, business, and aches and pains (of course) are all revealed at 120 decibels.

Every mobile phone call starts off with two obligatory questions. The first question is not 'How are you?', but 'Where are you?' The next time someone asks me that I am going to say 'I am clinging, now with one hand, onto the face of mount Kebnekaise'.

The next question is 'Is this a good time to call?' A reasonable question, I suppose, as some people do, in fact, have the annoying habit of answering only to inform you that you've called at a very inconvenient time.

> **"No, no, this is a great time to talk."**
> OVERHEARD IN THE GENTS´ TOILET. THE GUY STANDING NEXT TO ME, MOBILE IN ONE HAND, HIS MINI-MEMBER IN THE OTHER. NO CHANCE OF A PEE IN PEACE.

Mobile murder

Some people do all their business over the mobile phone while they're on their way to and from work. What they actually do when they're **at** work, goodness only knows. Have coffee breaks I suppose. These people make journeys on commuter trains particularly painful. *Hej Malin! Nej, jag sitter på tåget.* – 'I'm on the train'. Yes, you are, and please remember there are about twenty people within earshot who are not interested in what you are about to say. He, on the other hand, thinks everybody on board the train from Stockholm Central to Jordbro has chosen this very train for the chance to listen to the ins and outs of his work assignments. His constant babble is annoyingly interspersed with *Va?* – 'What?', *Det hörs dåligt* – 'Can't hear you' and *Hallo? Haaaaallo?* There is sweet silence as we thunder through a tunnel. *Hallo? Ah, du försvann! Vi åkte genom en tunnel.* –'You disappeared. We went through a tunnel'. I wish he would disappear, not necessarily through a tunnel, but down a black hole.

TELEPHONE SALES

In Sweden you can be rung up at any hour of the day, evening or weekend and they'll try to sell you anything from a newspaper subscription to a pair of underpants. To stop telephone salespeople in their tracks I always say 'That's great, I am really very interested but I'm busy right now so if you could leave your home number I'll call you back tonight at 11.30 pm.'

CHRISTMAS

Christmas is one of the main 'alcoholidays' of the year.

There are three stages in a young Swedish father's life – he believes in Father Christmas, he does not believe in Father Christmas, he **is** Father Christmas. On Christmas Eve a male member of the family, often the father, mysteriously disappears from the festivities and returns in the guise of Father Christmas himself, complete with horrific plastic mask with bushes of cotton wool sticking out. He dishes out the presents and then makes a hasty retreat, sweating rivers under his red and white costume with a cushion shoved up the front.

Swedes sing Christmas songs, like the well-known *Nu är det jul igen* – which, translated, means 'Oh no, it's Christmas again.'

If they're lucky Swedes can arrange what can be described as a *klämjul*. This is when the holidays Christmas, New Year and Twelfth Night all fall in the middle of three consecutive weeks. Swedes add on a few free days before and after and link them to the weekends. This way they stop work on 20 December and resume, say, around 10 January and *klämjulen*, an extended Christmas, is a fact.

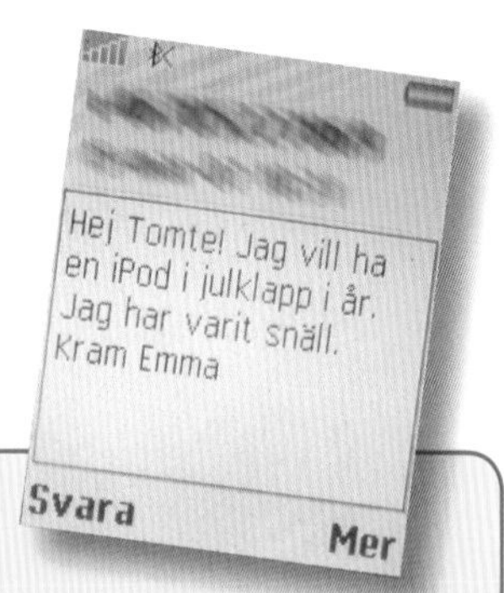

"Can't we just text him instead?"

MY SWEDISH GODDAUGHTER. I ASKED HER IF SHE WOULD LIKE TO WRITE A LETTER TO FATHER CHRISTMAS WITH HER WISH LIST. TYPICAL FOR HER GENERATION OF TECHNICALLY SUPER-LITERATE SWEDISH TODDLERS, THIS IS WHAT SHE REPLIED.

EVERYDAY SWEDISH
Lesson 6

Vann rätt låt?	van rett lawt?	(Lit: Did the right song win?) *Was it worth spending 2/3 of the annual SVT budget on choosing this song to represent Sweden in this year's Eurovision song Contest?*
– – –		(Lit: Complete silence) *(Pushing past in a queue at the supermarket check-out in Stockholm)*
Annars då?	annas då?	(Lit: Otherwise then?) *Apart from suffering the trials and tribulations of modern terrorism and personal traumas, I would like to inquire as to whether you are bearing up?*

THE NOBEL PRIZE

Any more tartelette au fromage de chèvre et sa garniture aux betteraves rouges anyone?

The spectacular award presentation ceremony with subsequent dinner and dance takes place each December. Most of us would give an arm and a leg for the chance to experience the splendour of the Nobel festivities. When that time does come, you'll be prepared. For here is a lesson in how to survive your first Nobel banquet.

French

How's your French? All the menus are written in French so brush it up, or, even better, sit next to the French ambassador. It's not the time to suddenly discover you're a vegetarian. One year the guests consumed 2,692 pigeon breasts. Ever thought of how they keep the bird population in check in Stockholm?

Camera

Be prepared for TV cameras to sweep past you and your fellow distinguished guests as you tuck into your *tartelette au fromage de chèvre et sa garniture aux betteraves rouges*. If you sense the camera zooming in then the TV commentators are probably commenting on you. This is not the time to have a piece of *délice de poire sur son bavarois chocolat-vanille accompagné d´un sorbet champagne-poire* hanging from your chin.

Dessert

The Bombe à la City Hall is the ice-crème de la ice-crème. Held high on large platters, the *glace Nobel – Glace au chocolat blanc et sorbet aux mûres sauvages* has to be served to 1,200 people and a family of royals within three minutes. Otherwise it starts melting and lady guests with bare shoulders are in for a rather chilling experience.

Conversation

Imagine you are seated next to a foreign dignitary. He may speak a language you understand, he may not. This is not the time to wish you had brought along your phrase book. If you feel that the conversation is drying up, make sure your neighbour has plenty of *Filet de cerf et son jus a la cannelle. Légumes d´automne grilles, chutney d´airelles rouges*. That'll keep him busy. If you're lucky then perhaps the total of 9,422 knives and forks being used against the 6,730 plates and bowls is so deafening that it doesn't really matter what you talk about.

Dance

Make sure you've practised your foxtrot, quickstep and tango so you too can twist and twirl among the dancing dignitaries. Dancing the night away helps to digest the *poularde rôtie et la sauce madère au foie gras*. The cameras are in full swing too and maybe they'll single you out and catch you in full jive just before you accidentally poke Baroness Beatrice von Stochen Bochen where no man has been before.

> **"In which subject?"**
> SIR WINSTON CHURCHILL, NOBEL PRIZE FOR LITERATURE IN 1953, WHEN HE HEARD THE NEWS HE HAD WON A NOBEL PRIZE.

ALLSÅNG

Each summer week there is 'Allsång på Skansen' on television. Roughly translated this means 'Let's all have a sing-song down at the open-air museum'.

A much-loved Swedish TV personality gets several thousand pensioners, teenagers and toddlers in the audience to sing old folk songs in more or less complete unison. The camera zooms in on Gunvor, 73, Lars, 42, Camilla, 17 and Felix, 4 1/2, as they put their heart into singing *'Kalle, Kalle, Kalle från Spånga'*. Viewers at home are expected to join in by reading the song texts on the screen. It's not unusual for the whole neighbourhood to be at it. It's terrific fun!

The big stars queue up to sing their latest and then lead a sing-along with the euphoric crowds. Carola, singer and saint, is an annual guest. In one of her wildest moments she has dived head-first into the ecstatic audience. She has since said she will not be repeating that particular party-trick as too many took the opportunity to get to know Carola in places she thought were private. *Allemansrätten*, the right of public access, does not apply to Carola, it seems.

SOCIALISING

Three things to remember:

1. If a stranger smiles at you in the street he is either *a*) drunk *b*) insane *c*) American
2. People may buy you a drink in November because they suddenly remember you bought them one last March.
3. Never just drop in unannounced. Arrange your last-minute visit several weeks in advance.

INVITATION 1

If you are lucky enough to be invited to a Swedish home your hosts will first expect you to take part in a highly intimate gesture. It's the tradition of taking off your shoes. If you're wearing high-heeled stilettos you'll immediately sink 10 cm down to floor level and your dress will hover around your ankles. The rest of us slide around the parquet in our socks giving it a good polish and shine. Meanwhile the hall looks like an abandoned shoe shop.

INVITATION 2

If it's your first visit your hosts will insist on taking you on a *husesyn* – a 'spontaneous' guided tour of every room, cupboard and corner of their home, which has been spotlessly cleaned three hours before you arrived. Before you know it they've whisked you into the bedroom for a good look at the matching bedside lamps and curtains and a quick bounce on their new Hästens bed. It's all part of their generous hospitality.

INVITATION 3

Having taken off your shoes and become acquainted with your hosts' sleeping quarters it's time for the welcoming ceremony. As guests you are given a drink and you're not expected to sip it until the host or hostess says *Välkomna!* That's the signal for everyone to hold up their glass and look each other in the eye. There's no need to stare. Sip your drink, hold your glass to your chest and repeat the procedure of looking everyone in the eye – just a glance is enough, and there's no need to wink or they'll think you fancy them.

On special occasions Swedes wipe their mouths on their national flag.

TOBACCO 1

Walk past any bar or restaurant nowadays and you're bound to see a small group of shivering souls huddled together just outside by the entrance. They take it in turns to say *Fy fan va' kallt!* – 'it's bloody cold!' Their survival depends on how quickly they get through a Blend Ultra-Mild. These die-hard smokers are simply enjoying their inter-course cancer sticks between main course and dessert in bitingly raw sub-zero temperatures.

TOBACCO 2

Not all Swedish tobacco goes up in smoke however. To the untrained eye some Swedes may appear to have a swollen upper lip and a case of seriously rotten teeth. This is *snus* – tobacco, water and salt in a miniature 'tea-bag' which they place under the upper lip. When it's not under the lip, you will find it in the urinals in the gents' toilet.

CONTACT ADS

Swedes love to be more average than most.

When they advertise for a partner Swedes often describe themselves as being just an 'ordinary guy', or a 'usual kind of girl' who is 'just like everyone else'. Whereas some of us strive to be someone special, Swedes in general try to be nobody in particular. It's a big turn-on to read about someone else's normality, especially if you're going to date them.

kvinna för tvåsamnet. (Sto 160708) T

En vanlig snubbe med glimten i ögat, rök- och spritfri. Söker vanlig tjej. Har allmänna intressen, gillar naturpromenader, mysiga hemmakvällar, tar gärna ett glas vin då och då. Barn är inget hinder. Kanske vi två? (Sto 160701)

Jag är en 29-årig kille med utländsk ...rund, ordnad ekonomi ...

"I am just an ordinary kind of guy with a sparkle in my eye, non-smoker, non-drinker. Looking for an ordinary kind of girl. Have general interests, like walks in the countryside, cosy evenings at home, like a glass of wine now and then. Children no problem. Maybe we two?"

RUDE SWEDISH

Swedes speaking Swedish can use the words 'bra', 'fart' and 'slut' in the same sentence without giggling.

They have a word *utfart*, meaning exit. The sign *Utfart dygnet runt* means the exit is in use 24 hours a day (!). There is also a word *infart* (!), which sounds pretty uncomfortable.

Amusing words in Swedish include words with *slut* – *slutbud, slutkontroll, slutsignal, slutstation* and *slutspurt*. Believe me, they are not what you first might think.

And then, of course, the word *sex*. If someone asks you for sex in Sweden, calm down. They are probably just asking you for half a dozen of whatever it is you've got.

For those wanting to improve their Swedish:
Bra = good, *fart* = speed, *slut* = sold-out, finished, end, *utfart* = a drive-out exit, *infart* = drive-in entrance, *slutbud* = final offer, final bid, *slutkontroll* = final check, *slutsignal* = final whistle, *slutstation* = end of the line, terminal (train etc), *slutspurt* = finishing spurt, run up.

TOILET

Going to the toilet is a naturally uncomplicated affair in Sweden.

Everybody does it and it's treated as a normal bodily function. Swedes can't understand why some foreigners try to disguise the fact that they have to 'spend a penny'... or, as we're in Sweden, spend a fortune. If you ask where Inga-Lill has gone you'll be informed: *hon sitter på muggen*, (approx: she is sitting on the pan). When Inga-Lill returns she will tell you where she has been – *på toa*, (literally 'on the toi'. They use the word so often they have to shorten it).

Swedes love being in the countryside enjoying a primitive, back-to-basics existence. This includes the times when a Swede's gotta do, what a Swede's gotta do. And they do it in the *utedass* – the outdoor lavatory. There are several types of outside loo, none of which is connected to the water mains. They're not for people with hang-ups like mine – if I can't flush it, I won't do it.

Now, let's get to the bottom of this. As I said, there are several types of outside john:

A chemical affair

You deliver into a container full of liquid chemicals. Your luggage is slowly attacked by hungry little micro-organisms which turns it into something unsightly and bio-degradable.

A 'mulltoa'

A dry loo filled with earth. Your luggage and pee is slowly mixed into the earth by a rotating arm (a mechanical one, not yours). You can use it as compost on your tomatoes several months later.

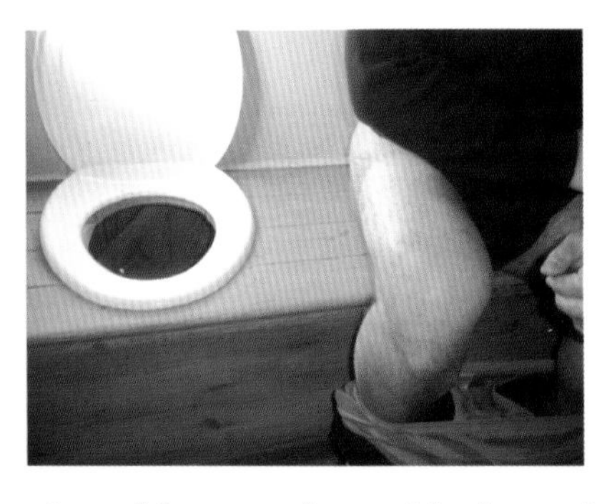

A wooden board with a hole in it

On which you sit, of course. Sometimes there are two holes where, once upon a time, you could sit and have a chat with the neighbour. You let the world fall out of your bottom into a bucket. No one ever talks about what happens to the bucket.

That, thank goodness, is the end of that.

Det gick bra! "That went well."

I WAS RECENTLY ASKED AT A DINNER PARTY BY THE LADY SITTING NEXT TO ME TO MIND HER BAG AS SHE WANTED TO GO TO THE LADIES. I EXPLAINED HOW SHE SHOULD GET THERE – UP THE STAIRS, TURN RIGHT, OPPOSITE THE LIFTS AND DOWN THE CORRIDOR. ON HER RETURN SHE PROMPTLY INFORMED ME ALL HAD GONE ACCORDING TO PLAN.

BLACK PLASTIC BAGS

While we're on the subject...

You rarely see dog's business on Swedish streets. Swedes pick it up. After the dog has emptied itself, the Swedish dog owner puts his hand into a small black plastic bag, bends down, picks up the steamy package and with a magical twist of the hand the dog's doo-doo ends up inside the bag. I have seen elderly, well-to-do ladies do this and put the black plastic bag, (for it is always black), plus contents directly into the pocket of their luxurious fur coat. I expect they then throw it away somewhere if they don't forget it's there.

Swedish doggy-bags.

CHILDREN

When a Swedish woman meets a partner nowadays the first thing she thinks is 'Is this the sort of man I want my children to spend their weekends with?'

Another way of dealing with children in a divorce is the *varannan vecka* arrangement. Many children in Sweden are shared equally by their parents – one week with *mamma* and the next with *pappa*. It's like moving from Brussels to Strasbourg every so often but on a smaller scale.

Swedes are very good with their kids. They bring them up like small adults. I am British. I tend to hit them. Swedes on the other hand talk

> **"Come quickly! Your kids and my kids are beating up our kids."**
>
> ONE SWEDISH WIFE TO HER PRESENT HUSBAND.

and reason with their children and give them a lot of responsibility from an early age. What impresses me most about Sweden is the way parents obey their children. There is a radio programme called *Fråga barnen* – Ask the children. Parents call and ask for advice on how long they can stay up in the evening.

Swedish teenagers, on the other hand, are just like teenagers in any other country. They express a burning desire to be different by dressing exactly alike.

EVERYDAY SWEDISH
Lesson 7

JA-je mensann!	yah – yeah mensann!	(Lit: yes, yeah, indeed!) *(Seemingly reserved for sports commentators only)*
Det är sjukt bra!	deh err shookt brar	(Lit: It's sickly good) *It's fantastic!*
Ja' ba' ...!	ya ba!	(Lit: I just...) *I leave my mouth open and you guess how I wish to express myself.*

MODESTY

We're best in the world. But we don't brag about it.

A world tennis-champion might admit: 'Well, I did manage to hit the ball over the net now and then.' A lone-sailor having crossed the Atlantic in a small boat confesses: 'Well, I suppose I did manage to keep afloat for most of the time.' A concert pianist acknowledges: 'I play a tune or two on the old grand piano. I do as well as I can, sometimes, perhaps ... but it depends.'

Successful people have just had a spot of luck and they just the do the best they can. 'I just had some luck and was able to build up a multinational company, win the World Championships in Scrabble, save the lives of thirty-two people from a burning inferno and win the Nobel Prize for chemistry.' *Man gör så gott man kan* – 'You just do the best you can.'

For they can't possibly succeed because they were better than anybody else, can they?

Det är ba' å åk – "You just get on and ski".

THE ULTIMATE IN SWEDISH MODESTY: THE WORLD CHAMPION SKIER INGEMAR STENMARK ONCE EXPLAINED THE SECRET OF WINNING SO MANY INTERNATIONAL SKIING TROPHIES.

UNSWEDISH

How to be unmistakably Swedish.

An American saying 'Gee, today I'm gonna go all un-American' would be classified as unpatriotic and put on the terrorist list. A Brit saying 'How wonderfully un-British' would be sent to the Tower for high treason. A Frenchman saying 'Today I will eat un-French food' would cause the farmers to take to the streets of Paris.

Swedes, believe it or not, sometimes use the word *osvensk* (un-Swedish) to mean something exciting, colourful, and lively. But that doesn't necessarily mean that the word *svensk* (Swedish) means the opposite as in 'This is Lars, he is Swedish, dull, drab and dreary.' The word *svensk* (Swedish) can be used positively, especially in terms of Swedish quality, Swedish reliability and Swedish honesty. However, when they are in one of their self-

Fem frågor/
till Per Holmer,
författaren som fått lysande recensioner för romanen "Svindel". Den beskrivs som en av de absolut bästa romanerna på senare år, som en tvålopera i mycket positiv mening, som underhållande, rik på personer och associationer, osvensk, för att bara nämna några av lovorden.

Per Holmer, author, has received brilliant reviews for his novel "Vertigo". It has been heralded as one of the best novels of recent years, like a quality soap-opera, entertaining, rich in characters and associations, unswedish – to mention just some of the praise it has received.

critical moods, Swedes spit out the words *typiskt svenskt!* (typically Swedish!) to describe something or someone as bureaucratic, inflexible and indecisive. So if someone introduces you to Lars and says 'This is Lars, he is typically Swedish', then you know what kind of person you are dealing with.

THE MEANING OF 'LAGOM'

An excess of moderation.

At the local swimming baths part of the pool is often cordoned off for ladies' water gymnastics. Another part is reserved for the under fives. Although you pay the full entrance fee you are often not allowed to use the whole pool. The long narrow section on the far right or far left of the pool is reserved for *motionssim* – a word difficult to translate but which means swimming for exercise.

In this section everybody swims the same stroke at the same speed. They swim up one side of the narrow stretch, turn at the end and then back along the other side, in a kind of elongated circle. Round and round they go. In perfect symmetry. No-one swims any faster than anyone else. Any newcomers into the circle slide down into the

Round and round we go. A sign by the pool to show how to do it.

water, without a splash, and join the unbroken chain of Swedes swimming head to toe in complete synchronicity.

Nobody gets their head wet. They swim a slow version of the breast stroke, with head held high and minimal splashing. It's curious, not to say calming, to watch.

It's like suddenly discovering the meaning of life. For this must be the meaning of *lagom*.

LAUNDRY

Swedes have a reputation for being as calm as a cucumber.

That is, it seems, until they do their washing. A recent survey shows that thefts and threats in the communal laundry in the basement of apartment blocks is part of everyday life.

Every fifth Swede has ended up in an argument

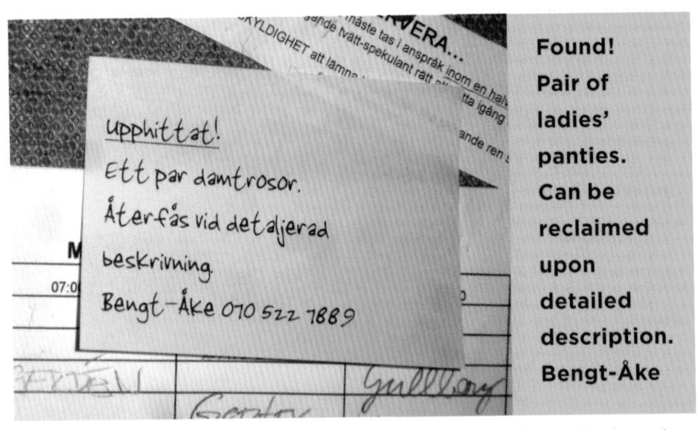

In my apartment block we still pin small notices on the notice board outside the laundry if we want to communicate with our neighbours.

in the 'washing cottage' as the laundry is affectionately called. Lack of respect for others' washing times and failing to tidy up afterwards are the most common complaints. 11 % say they have actually been attacked. It's not just the washing that's dirty it seems.

The majority (21%) claim that a clogged-up tumble-dryer filter is the cause of harsh words among neighbours who, apart from fluff and pubic hair in the filter, normally have very little in common.

BALCONY

The ultimate in Stockholm is to own an apartment with a balcony. In Stockholm there is what one might describe as 'balcony apartheid'. The city is divided into the 'haves' and the 'have-nots'. The haves are further divided into the 'I-have-a-balcony-facing-south' and the 'I-get-the-sun-between-8-and-10.30-every-morning'.

There are two occasions when you will see Swedes out on their balcony.

1) It's February, minus 15 degrees and they're dressed like the Michelin tyre man trying to hold a cigarette between what looks like boxing gloves and raise it to a pair of blue lips.
2) It's May, plus 15 degrees and they're stretched out on their balcony trying to get a head start on their tan.

STATISTICS

42.7 % of statistics are made up on the spot and 43.3% of them are meaningless.

You try telling that to the Swedes. 100% of them will disagree. Swedes rely on statistics.

A casual browse through any newspaper or a half-hour's listen to the radio will provide you with more or less very relevant statistics. Here is a selection of statistical facts I have been fed with just this morning:

- The people of Stockholm drank a total of 1 731 660 litres of spirits last year.
- 93 people were injured on trampolines in the Umeå area from 1995 – 2007, an increase of 63%.
- 3 514 000 people watched Donald Duck on Christmas Eve at 3 pm. This includes 41.6% of those aged between 60 and 99.
- There are 1.4 inhabitants per square kilometre in Berg kommun, which is the municipality of Mountain.
- 90% of crimes occur after the offenders have eaten some form of bread.

So, now it's been proved. Eating bread makes you criminal.

SURVEYS

To get the statistics you need to conduct surveys.

Swedes are invited to take part in countless surveys. The results are often published the next day in the daily newspapers. This web-based survey asks 'Do you answer honestly in surveys on the net?' 21% give the answer that they do not take part in web surveys.

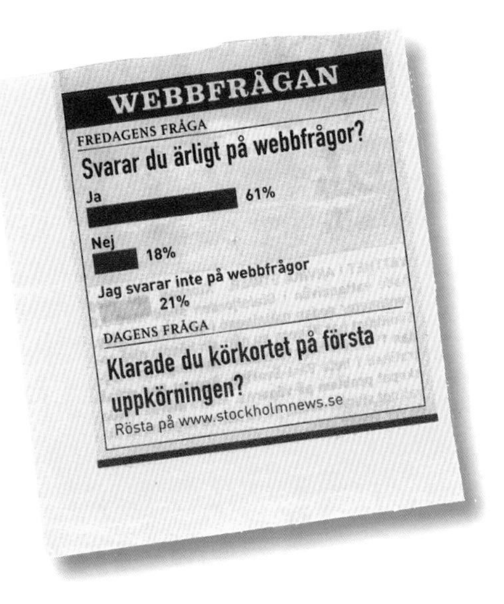
WEBBFRÅGAN

FREDAGENS FRÅGA

Svarar du ärligt på webbfrågor?

Ja 61%

Nej 18%

Jag svarar inte på webbfrågor 21%

DAGENS FRÅGA

Klarade du körkortet på första uppkörningen?

Rösta på www.stockholmnews.se

SINFUL SWEDEN

Forget it.

Once, not so long ago, the Swedes had a healthy attitude to nakedness – it was seen, but not looked at. The evening papers have put a stop to all that and, in a manner which up to now has been truly hypocritically Anglo-Saxon, have turned sex and skin into something smutty and shameful.

The evening press invented a word *nakenchock* – the shock and horror of showing something they think should be covered up. But they also come up with huge headlines such as *Mina bröst sprack!* – My breasts exploded! *Hennes bröst växte under tv-sändningen* – Her breasts grew during the TV broadcast and *Svenska kvinnor talar ut om sina silikonbröst!* – Swedish women speak out about their silicon

breasts! The British tabloids would be envious.

You don't actually see any of these breasts as there is a complete nipple-stop in all Swedish media. Showing the smooth, soft, round things in their entirety would be considered sexist and exploiting the female body, wouldn't it?

No boobs

A retail company advertised bras, one of its main products. Ads outdoors and in the media showed close-ups of a woman in a black, fairly innocent bra. The slogan read 'We love all boobs!' Within days Stockholm Transport had forced the company to remove the text as this could offend the frail few who got it into their heads that 'boobs' was vulgar. Yes, you may have to read that last sentence again but it is true. The perfectly safe and round-sounding word was classified as sexist and disturbing. According to a survey 9.8%, of the 650 000 who travel on the Stockholm metro each day were of the opinion that the word was degrading. Thank goodness for the 90% who, presumably, all love boobs!

'Tootsies' for toes, 'pinkies' for little fingers and 'cheeks' for buttocks are some cute names in English for other parts of the human anatomy – just in case the guardians of public morality, Stockholm Taliban Transport, wants to ban those in future too.

Problems with exploding boobs all over the plac

Fredrik in underwear

The city planning committee banned an enormous ad (360 sq. m) with the gorgeously beautiful Swedish football player Fredrik Ljungberg and the ravishingly super-duper looking Natalia Vodianova. They were lying in a stylish, sensual position and were dressed only, of course, in their Calvin Klein undies. The ad had been shown all over the world. In Stockholm, however, those policing public morals were out in force and said *Usch!* and banned it from ever being put up.

EUROVISION SONG CONTEST

The ESC – the everlasting song contest.

In the red seventies, the loony left succeeded in forcing Sweden to pull out of the ESC altogether. It was capitalist, competitive and corrupt.

Not so today. In the garden of SwEden the run-up to the ESC is the biggest television event of the year. There are not one but five spectacular heats culminating in the phenomenal final to decide the song to represent la Suède in the actual ESC later in the spring.

In the UK, the British song is selected during a 30 minute programme squeezed in between

Emmerdale Farm and the 6 o'clock news. The singers range from those who failed their first audition on 'Idol' to the unemployable. To take part in the ESC is considered to be as honourable as taking part in your own funeral.

Not so in Sweden. To take part is a national honour. Indeed there are some artists who do little else but turn up each year with a 'make-over light' of the song they sang the previous year, with lyrics by Pingela Fling Forsmun. Then there are the really big names in Swedish entertainment who come in as 'jokers' and crown their careers by showing the likes of Jimmy Jansson and Sanna Nielsen that they might just as well not have bothered.

Each Saturday in February child allowances are used up as families ring in over and over again to vote for their favourite songs and the next day the evening newspapers give detailed coverage on pages 30, 31, 36, 37, 38, 39, 40, 41, 42, 43, 46, 58 and 60.

"Le Royaume Uni : trois points – three pints."

MOST BRITS WOULD BE HAPPIER WITH THE BEER.

CAROLA

Carola and her wind-machine have represented Sweden three times.

The first time she sang in the final, 84% of the Swedish population watched her come third. That's almost the entire population apart from the ultra-left, the sick and the homeless.

Det var Guds vilja att jag kom trea "It was God's will that I came third."

BIBLE-CLUTCHING CAROLA, SWEDEN'S EUROVISION QUEEN, THINKS GOD HAD NOTHING BETTER TO DO THAT EVENING THAN WATCH THE EUROVISION SONG CONTEST.

GAMBLING

Are Swedes passionate gamblers? You bet!

The Swedes have a curious attitude towards wealth. They desire it for themselves but begrudge it to others. And so, not surprisingly, there are very few methods of acquiring wealth of which they approve. Gambling is one of them.

The largest gaming company (turnover SEK 20 billion) is owned by the state, and its forceful marketing urges Swedes to take up and keep up the habit. It encourages Swedes to buy a whole array of scratchcards, take a chance on the lottery, and bet on the horses. It entices them to play poker, bingo, and pick'n click on the internet – and the football pools, the lottery with the Dream Prize and even more bingo on their mobile.

Addict

The odds are that you'll end up an addict. But fear not! The state-owned company is a caring company. You are advised not to be silly and gamble away your house, car and family in one go. If you do go so far as to stake your mother-in-law the company tells you nicely that you probably need help. To start with, try to ignore their un-avoidable aggressive marketing campaigns on the telly, in the press and on every billboard up and down the country. I'll bet you a *Trisslott* (scratch-card) you won't succeed.

In Sweden the state is croupier, casino manager, and gambling addiction therapist all in one. Most of the proceeds and profits from the Swedish mania for gambling go straight into the state piggy bank. So, the more you lose, the richer the welfare state. Which of course needs the money to care for people it has led into temptation.

> **"There are few things in this world more comforting, however, than an unhappy lottery winner."**
>
> A FRIEND OF MINE WHO HAS A DOSE OF THAT SWEDISH ENVY THING.

POLITICS

Swedish politicians are like politicians everywhere else. They are always there when they need you.

At election times they know that it is not enough to have every intelligent person in the country voting for them. They also need a majority. Over 80% of the electorate vote and they are divided into the blues, the reds and the 'don't-knows'. One day the 'don't-knows' will get in, and then what will happen?

Riksdagen, the Swedish parliament, is like any other parliament. Somebody gets up and says nothing. Nobody listens and then everybody takes turns to get up and disagree.

So how do Swedish politicians differ from other politicians in the world?

In the USA, Presidential candidates pat babies on their heads. In the UK, British politicians pat animals. In France they pat farmers. In Sweden, politicians tend to plant trees.

They like to be called by their first names. This way they project the ultimate in Swedishness: *jag är som folk är mest* – 'I am just like any Tom, Dick or Harry' ... or in this case, Fredde, Mona or Lasse.

At election times they take part in programmes

called *Partiledarduell* at prime time on the telly and on the radio. This is an organised duel (this is Sweden, after all) where they let the leaders of the political parties loose in a studio and tell them to thrash it out. It's the left in the red corner and the right in the blue corner and with an artillery of insults and verbal abuse the battle begins.

DRIVING

Survey after survey proves that Swedes are good drivers.

They are so good that they are able to hold a cell phone in their right hand up to their right ear, hold the steering wheel with their left, indicate simultaneously, quickly move the cell phone over to the left hand, change gear with the now-free right hand, hold steering wheel with left elbow, look into the rear mirror (oh sweet miracle), use right hand to turn left into a street crowded with cars, cyclists and pedestrians, and at the same time take part in an involved conversation – and it's all perfectly legal.

Swedes are also safe drivers.

And there is safety in numbers. That's why they all drive in the middle of a three lane highway. Regardless of whether they are crawling along at snail's pace or breaking the sound barrier, they stick to the middle lane. It makes no difference if they're driving a car, a bus or a dirty great truck – the middle lane is a magnet. Young man, middle-aged man in a cap, woman, Swedish or foreign – they all do it, they clog up the middle lane. The inside lane is usually empty apart from the cars coming onto the motorway. These immediately, for some reason only known to the drivers themselves, seize the first opportunity to squeeze into the middle lane, leaving a perfectly empty lane on the near side. The occasional less patient driver overtakes in the outside lane, only to return as soon as his chance arises to the choc-a-bloc middle lane. Half of the drivers are heavily engaged in a conversation on their hand-held mobiles because that is clearly more important than concentrating on the motorway traffic, isn't it?

"One way to solve the traffic problem is to keep all the cars not paid for off the street."

PEOPLE SAY THERE ARE TOO MANY CARS IN STOCKHOLM AND THEREFORE THE CONGESTION TAX HAS BEEN INTRODUCED. AN ENVIRONMENTALIST HAD ANOTHER IDEA.

EVERYDAY SWEDISH
Lesson 8

Shit också!	Shit oxo	(Lit: Shit as well) *Swedes borrow Anglo-Saxon swear words although they have perfectly good ones of their own – like hell, devil and forest as in 'go to the forest'.*
Typ	Tüüp	(Lit: Type) *Something like that. Sort of.* As in *'Are you enjoying this book?' Typ.*
Bjuda på sig själv	b-yewda poh say shelv	(Lit: to offer oneself!) *The laugh is on me and I'm secure enough and brave enough to take it.* *

* A marvellous Swedish quality which is particularly useful when they read a book like this.

CYCLISTS IN STOCKHOLM

Deaf, dumb and blind.

Cyclists of the world have obviously united. Whether in Stockholm, Moscow or Bombay they have less road sense that a retarded rabbit. They may be friendly to the environment but that's where it stops. They believe they have the god-given right to ignore anything that vaguely resembles good traffic manners. They collectively perform kamikaze attacks on anything in their path. In Stockholm they don't see the point of stopping at red lights. Either that or they're all colour-blind. Point this out to them as they whisk past like a mosquito on speed and you're likely to be shown the middle finger. It isn't so much the cyclists that need a helmet but the rest of us.

PARKING

There must have been a time in Stockholm when it cost more to run a car than park it.

The Swedish Road Administration is very generous with its signs and signposts. On average there is a sign every five metres usually telling you what you can't do. You may not park 10 m from a corner or from a zebra crossing, facing the opposite direction, on certain days, and at certain times. Why does anybody bother stopping at all?

If you really must stop your car, here is a place. But don't be too quick to shout Eureka. It's going to cost you the equivalent of an arm and a leg between 9 am and 5 pm. After 5 o'clock it's free except that you'd stand a greater chance of finding a parking space on the moon than in the streets of Stockholm.

Now, find a ticket machine. There is one across the road, 20 metres down the street. Estimate, to the nearest minute, how long you intend to stay. Put in money or swipe card. Hopefully you'll have the right card. Pull out ticket. Take back to car and continue reading signs.

The ticket in your hand is white. The sign says it should be blue or red. Swear. Discover another ticket machine just four metres away in the opposite direction on your side of the road. The blue and red ticket machine.

Wednesday nights is not a good time to stay over as that's the night the road cleaners come. Even when they don't, you're still likely to get a parking fine because you have disobeyed the sign. If you happen to be a resident in the area called *Sö*, you can ignore the second sign down but not the yellow sign immediately above as that's the Wednesday night curfew.

The arrows stipulate you may park from here to there only.

Lars was driving in a sweat down a street in Stockholm because he had an important meeting and he couldn't find a parking space.

Looking up to heaven, secular Lars said, "Please God, help me. If you find me a parking place I will believe in you, go to church every Sunday for the rest of my life and give up weekend drinking."

Miraculously, a parking place appeared.

Lars looked up again and said, "Never mind, I found one."

ROAD SIGNS 1

The Swedish Roads Administration has decreed that there are to be no signs in English along Swedish roads. They refer to a European agreement dating back to the 1970s. And we all know which country follows ancient agreements regardless if the world has since moved on.

This means that if foreign tourists want somewhere to stay in Sweden they will first have to go on a crash course in Swedish. The sign B&B or Bed and Breakfast is not allowed. Foreign tourists are advised to look for signs with *Rum och frukost.*

This is interesting as I have seen other signs in English which have been allowed to stay up. *Bad Camping** for example. I wonder if they got any foreign visitors.

* *Bad* = bathing

The word Stop in Swedish is spelled *Stopp*. However on their stop signs they use the English spelling with just one ‘p’. *Stop* in Swedish means a beer tankard. Imagine having a sign for beer mugs at the end of roads in your country.

ROAD SIGNS 2

We love boobs!

Keep to middle
lane only

Statistics en route

Absolut Systembolaget

Warning! Swedes in action

Play Lotto here

Warning! *Nakenchock* ahead.

Welcome to Switzerl...
... Sweden!

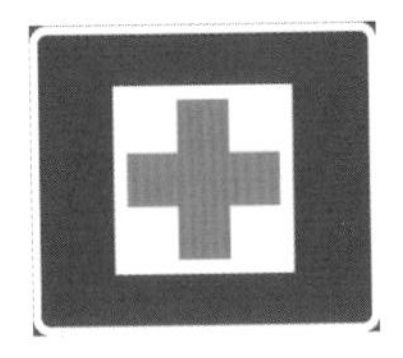

Warning! Politician
planting tree

Maths test

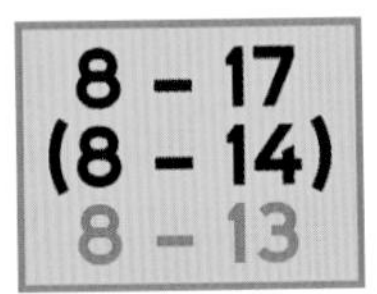

Warning! German tourists

Warning! *Beslutsimpotens*

Tennis court ahead

Meeting in progress

Warning! Anarchy.
All signs removed.

Hej mina vänner!

Självklart kan jag inte påstå att alla svenskar är punktliga. Jag känner en svensk som har en sämre tidsuppfattning än en mask. Det är också klart att jag inte kan påstå att alla svenskar någon gång har torkat sig om munnen med en servett med svensk flagga på. Och jag erkänner, det finns uppenbarligen svenskar som ogärna står i kö. Vissa svenskar fattar beslut på löpande band, och det finns andra som avskyr bara tanken på Melodifestivalen. Det finns förmodligen också de som gillar myggor.

Men denna bok innehåller inga sanningar. Den består av en samling betraktelser som jag gjort under mina fina år i Sverige.

Man ser inte världen som den är, man ser världen som man själv är.

Colin Moon

If you wish to order this book, please visit
www.mercuri-kongress.se

Garden of SwEden är utgiven av Mercuri Kongress AB.
Boken kan beställas på *www.mercuri-kongress.se*
eller på 08-26 46 02.

Mercuri Kongress AB och Colin Moon
har också givit ut *Lazy Dog – lathund
för dig som talar mycket engelska på telefon* och
*e-right@work – lathund för dig som
skriver mycket mejl på engelska.*

Photographer: Leif Jacobsson
www.leifjacobsson.com
Cover and graphic design: John Eyre
www.johneyre.com
ISBN 978-91-976222-1-9

Wikströms, Uppsala 1070409